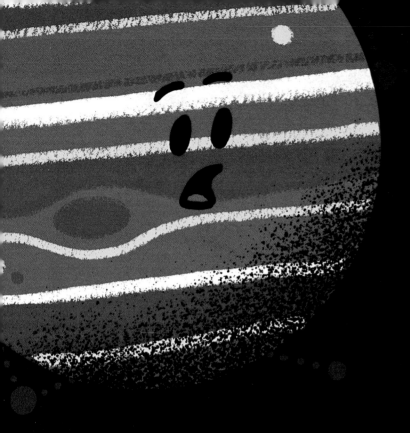

To Mom and Dad: the best parents
in the known universe—M. R.

To my son, Hezekiah
—B. W.

OH NO, ASTRO!

Matt Roeser Illustrated by Brad Woodard

SCHOLASTIC INC.

Everyone knows that asteroids are a rather rambunctious group.

BASH!

CR SH

SMASH!

NO LOITERIN[G]

Well . . . *most* asteroids.

All Astro wanted was for his personal
outer space to be respected—as it had been
for millions of years.

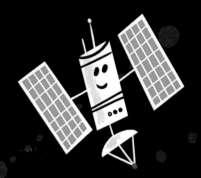

"Greetings, celestial wanderer,"
said Astro to an approaching satellite.

"Please keep your distance. You stay
in your orbit and I'll stay in mine.

It's one of the core rules
of the cosmos, you know."

"And yet, you've come closer."

"GOOD GRAVITY!

You've struck me!"

Astro was understandably distraught.

But before he could point out to the satellite that it had done considerable damage to one of his favorite craters, he began to spin.

"Pluto's revenge! That rotating rogue seems to have knocked me off orbit!"

"This.

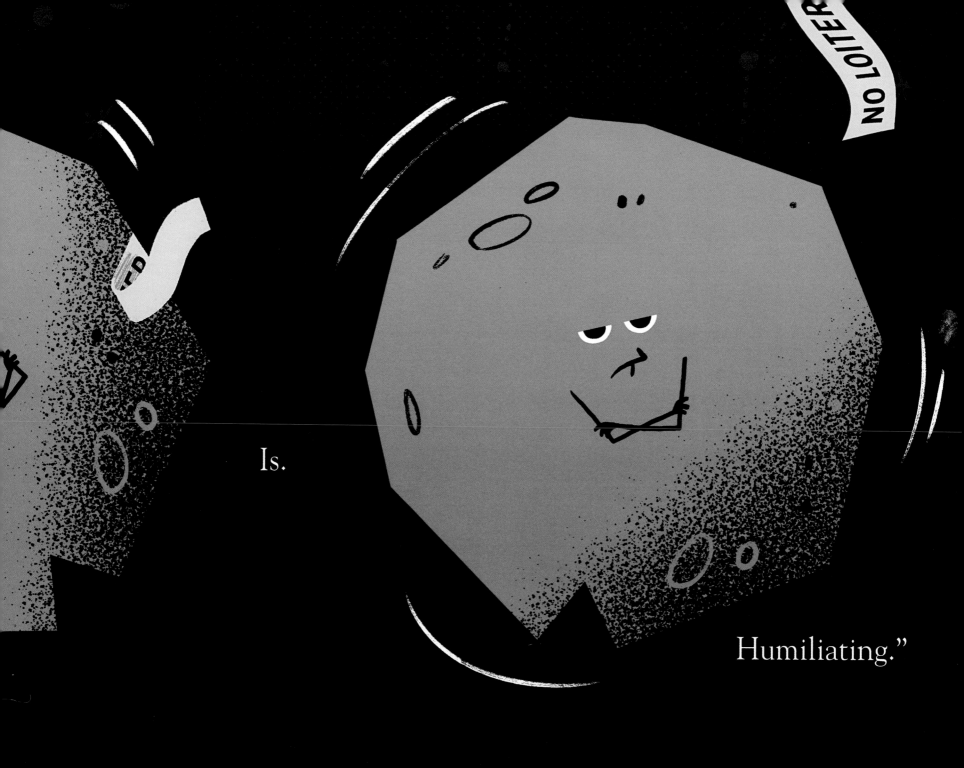

Astro found himself in unknown territory.

*"When an asteroid leaves its orbit, it hurtles through space
on an unpredictable path, reaching unstoppable speeds . . ."*

"Why, I'd *never!*"

But he did.

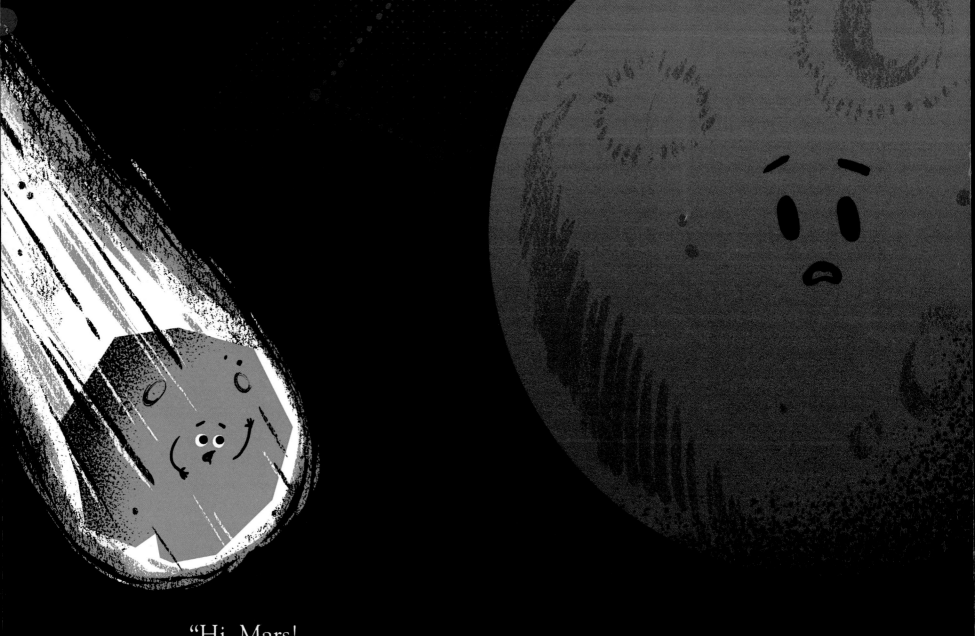

"Hi, Mars!

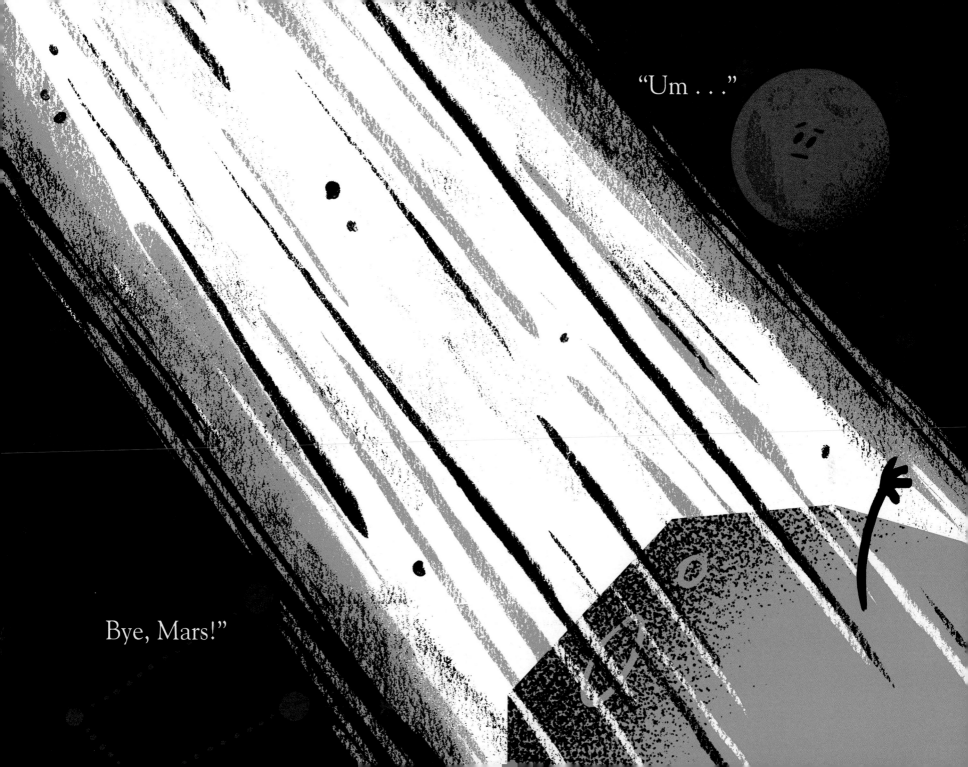

Meanwhile, an Earth girl named Nova
was enjoying a quiet night of stargazing,
when something caught her eye.

"Pardon . . .

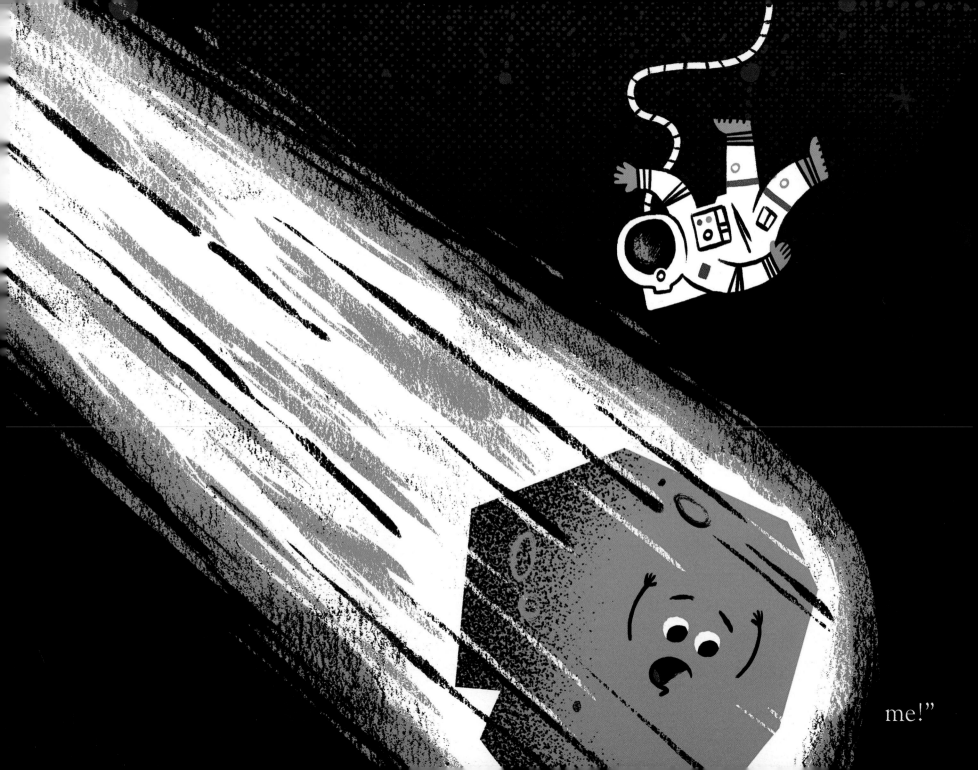

me!"

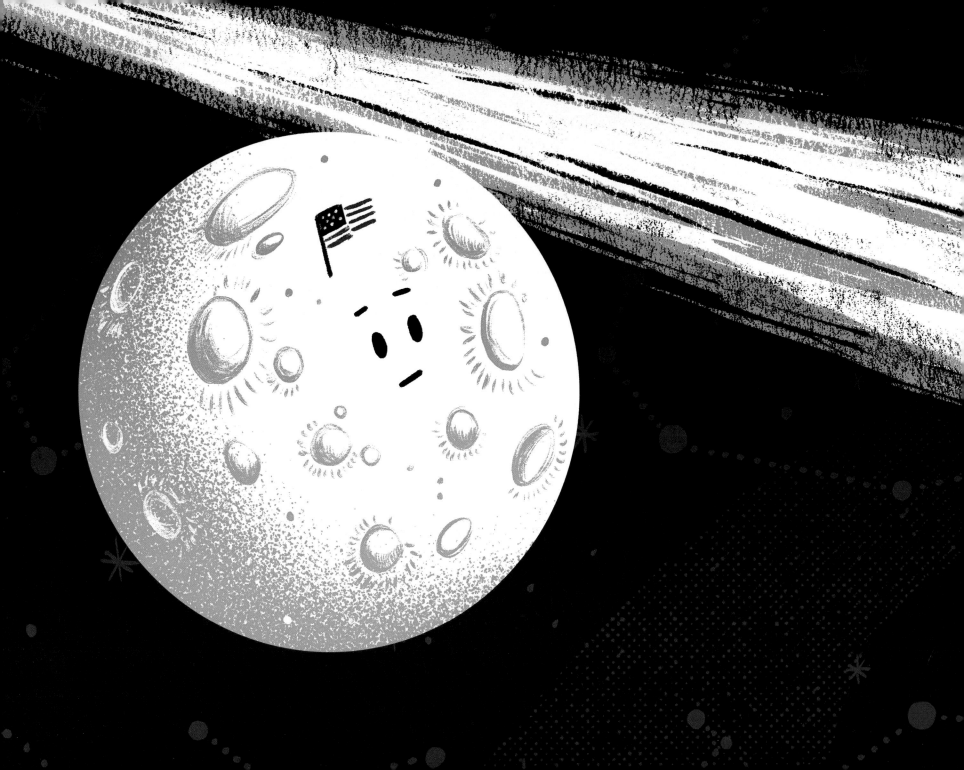

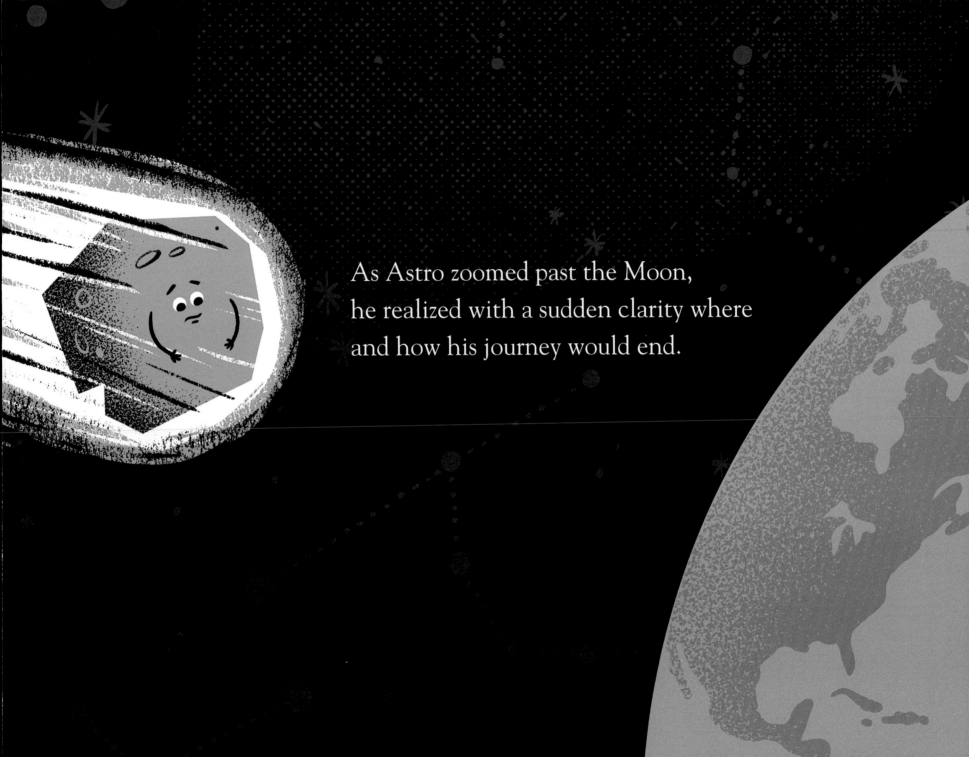

As Astro zoomed past the Moon,
he realized with a sudden clarity where
and how his journey would end.

"I don't like confrontation!"

Astro began to break apart as he entered Earth's atmosphere.

"It tickles!"

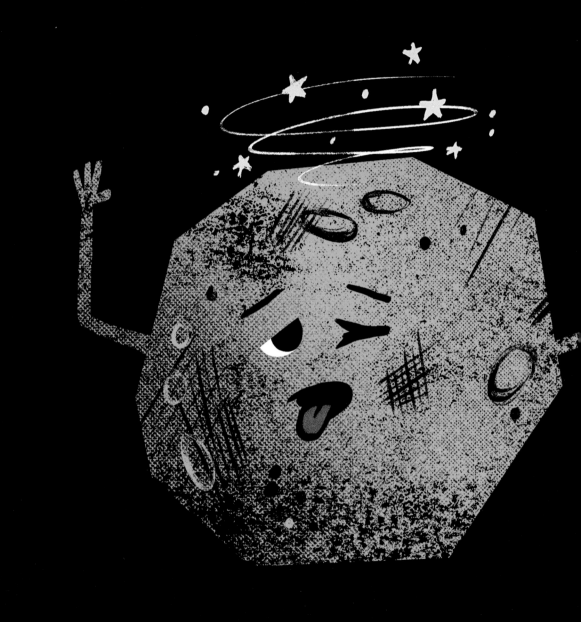

Astro opened one eye. Then the other.

He was certainly smaller, but still in one piece.

"My stars," he muttered. "Dare I say that was . . .

"FUN?!"

"What on Earth shall we do next?!"

A SELECTION OF SPACE FACTS

taken from the
Manual of the Cosmos,
2nd edition

Where are the asteroids in the solar system?

Asteroids like Astro live in the region of the solar system called the asteroid belt, which, contrary to popular belief, is not holding up our galaxy's pants. Located between the orbits of Mars and Jupiter, the asteroid belt contains between one and two million of these rocky fragments in varying sizes. With such a large population, collisions between asteroids frequently occur. No wonder Astro kept to himself!

What are satellites, and why does one hit Astro?

A satellite is a machine we've made down here on Earth and launched into space to send information back to us. The first satellite ever sent into space, back in 1957, was Sputnik 1. Since then, over 6,500 have been sent into orbit! But they don't all stay there. Some stop working and become classified as space debris. Some fall back to Earth. Others accidentally bump into asteroids. Of all of the satellites up in the sky, about 1,000 are still operational. They provide information on the weather, allow us to do cool things on our cell phones, and serve as the villain in picture books.

What exactly is an orbit?

Have you ever wondered why planets, moons, and stars don't just crash into each other as they move around in space? Much like a toy train on a track, planets and other celestial objects move on a path called an orbit. Orbits come in different shapes, but most are elliptical, which is a fancy word for oval-shaped. Asteroids have a fairly typical circular path, but orbits, like certain aunts, can also be highly eccentric.

Astro yells some silly things.
What does "Pluto's revenge!" mean?

Today there are eight planets in our solar system: Mercury, Venus, Earth, Mars, Jupiter, Saturn, Uranus, and Neptune. But until 2006, there was a ninth planet! And it was called Pluto. That year, scientists started picking on Pluto because it was so small (even smaller than our moon). After they argued for a while, they officially made it pack its bags, declaring it a dwarf planet. Pluto is still in therapy.

How does Mars compare to Earth?

Even though Mars is our planetary neighbor, living there would be quite different from living on Earth. Not only would you have to wear a space suit to breathe the different air, but instead of seeing green land, blue skies, and water, you'd have an endless view of red

dust storms. With the difference in gravity, you'd weigh a third of what you weigh on Earth! And a day on Mars lasts forty minutes longer than a day on Earth, so while you'll have more time, you'll probably spend it emptying all that dust from your space boots.

Why *is* Mars red?

As delicious as it would be, Mars is not covered in ketchup. Instead, the Red Planet gets its nickname from the fact that it's coated in an iron-rich dust that is rusty red in color. Intense storms and ancient volcanoes swirl the dust around, continually changing Mars's surface. When the orbits of Earth and Mars bring them close to each other, Mars appears an even *brighter* red in the night sky. One other theory: Mars is just blushing because she has a crush on Astro!

Is there really a flag on the Moon?

Yes. In 1969 American astronauts Neil Armstrong and Buzz Aldrin were the first people to ever set foot on the Moon, and marked the occasion by planting a US flag on its surface. However, if you saw that flag today, you might be surprised. That's because over time, it's likely that the flag has been completely bleached white by the intense UV radiation of the sun's rays hitting the Moon's surface. If you ever visit the Moon, bring a new flag, or at least take a selfie with the old one.

Why does Astro go from being so very big to being so very small?

Surrounding our planet is a layer of gases which we call the atmosphere. When an object, such as Astro, enters the atmosphere at a very high speed, its temperature rises (up to 3,000 degrees Fahrenheit!). This causes parts of Astro to disintegrate as he heats up, resulting in a rapid loss of mass (and most of his personal belongings). As his outer layer is continuously vaporized, his path glows and burns like a shooting star. By the time Astro crashes into Nova's backyard, he's lost most of his mass (but still has *all* of his sass).

What is the difference between an asteroid, a meteor, and a meteorite?

Everyone knows that Astro is an asteroid. But at different points in his journey to Earth, scientists technically have different names for what he is. He starts out as an asteroid in the asteroid belt. Once he begins burning up in the Earth's atmosphere, he's called a meteor. And once he survives falling through the Earth's atmosphere and crashes into Nova's backyard, he's called a meteorite. It's enough to confuse anyone, so you can just call him Astro.

How many meteorites hit Earth each year?

Around 500 meteorites reach the Earth's surface every year, but, of those, only around five ever make it to scientists to study. This is mostly because unless someone has seen one fall from the sky, meteorites look a lot like everyday rocks. You might even have some in your backyard! Of the 50,000 meteorites found on Earth to date, 99.8 percent are believed to have come from the asteroid belt. So keep your eyes peeled for falling debris—you just might spot one of Astro's former acquaintances!

Source:

www.nasa.gov

Suggested reading:

The assortment of amazing science books by Franklyn M. Branley.

First Space Encyclopedia from DK Publishing, 2008.

National Geographic Little Kids First Big Book of Space by Catherine D. Hughes, illustrated by David A. Aguilar, National Geographic Children's Books, 2012.

This Is the Way to the Moon by Miroslav Sasek, Universe Publishing, 2009.

Special thanks to Tim Federle, without whom Astro wouldn't have soared.
—M. R.